Library of Old English and Medieval Literature

# THE ART OF
# GEOFFREY CHAUCER

# SIR ISRAEL GOLLANCZ
## MEMORIAL LECTURE

# THE ART OF
# GEOFFREY CHAUCER

by JOHN LIVINGSTON LOWES

*Read* December 3, 1930

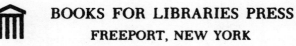

## BOOKS FOR LIBRARIES PRESS
### FREEPORT, NEW YORK

First Published 1930
Reprinted 1970

STANDARD BOOK NUMBER:
8369-5315-0

LIBRARY OF CONGRESS CATALOG CARD NUMBER:
70-114910

PRINTED IN THE UNITED STATES OF AMERICA

# SIR ISRAEL GOLLANCZ MEMORIAL LECTURE

# THE ART OF GEOFFREY CHAUCER

### By JOHN LIVINGSTON LOWES

#### *Read* December 3, 1930

THIS is the first lecture on the Foundation which bears the name of Sir Israel Gollancz. He was my friend, as he was the friend of countless other scholars, and he gave to his friendships the same warm humanity that he brought to his scholarship. And it is fitting that the theme of this lecture, chosen before his death, should be the poet whose learning, more than that of any other, was also irradiated and mellowed by his humanity.

———

MY subject, as I have announced it, is a theme for a volume, but titles can seldom be brief and specific at once. I mean to limit myself to an attempt to answer—and that but in part—a single question: What, aside from genius, *made* the poet of the greater CANTERBURY TALES? How, in a word, did he master a technique at its height so consummate that it often seems not to be art at all, but the effortless play of nature? And by what various roads did he travel in passing from his earlier to his later themes? That twofold evolution, of technique and subject matter, is singularly rich in human as well as literary interest, and it is worth the effort to reconstruct, as far as possible, its processes.

One of the glories of English poetry has been the interpenetration in it of personal experience—call it for brevity life, if you will—and of books. Through the one, poetry acquires its stamp of individuality; through the other it is dipped in the quickening stream of tradition which has flowed through the work of all the poets from Homer and pre-Homeric days until now. The continuity of poetry, through its participation in that deep and perpetually broadening current, is a fact perhaps more important than the newness of the channels through which from time to time it flows. The greatest poetry is, indeed, steeped in the poet's own experience and coloured by the life of his times. But it also participates in a succession almost apostolic, in which there is an authentic if incorporeal laying on of hands:

> Go, litel book . . .
>
> . . . no making thou n'envye,
> But subgit be to alle poesye;
> And kis the steppes, wher-as thou seest pace
> Virgile, Ovyde, Omer, Lucan, and Stace.

That is from the close of a masterpiece which is at once sheer Chaucer and an embodiment of the tradition of the elders from Homer through the Middle Ages to a contemporary fellow poet, Boccaccio; and I suspect that no one in the long and splendid line of English poets more strikingly exemplifies than Geoffrey Chaucer the characteristic interplay, in great verse, of life and books. For he was, on the one hand, a widely experienced, busy, and versatile man of affairs, and he was also one of the most omnivorous readers in that company of glorious literary cormorants who have enriched English letters. Had he been either without the other—had there been lacking either the immediate and manifold contacts with life, or the zest of a *helluo librorum*—he would doubtless still have been a poet. But in that case not one of the poems by which he is known could even remotely have been what it is. Let me, then, rehearse as necessary background, even at the risk of seeming for the moment to abandon poetry, a few of the familiar facts.

No other English poet, in the first place, has approached Chaucer in the breadth and variety of his immediate, personal experience of life. For no other English poet—to pack a lifetime into a list—was a page in a royal household and for years Yeoman or Esquire at Court; was captured while in military service, and then ransomed by the King; was sent to Flanders, France, and Italy on half a dozen delicate and important diplomatic missions, involving royal marriages, commercial treaties, and treaties of peace; was

Controller of the Customs and Subsidy of wools, hides, and wool-fells, and also Controller of Petty Customs, in the port of London; was Justice of the Peace, and member of Parliament; Clerk of the King's Works, with exacting duties and wide powers, at Westminster Palace, the Tower of London, the Castle of Berkhampstead, and at seven of the royal manors, with their gardens, mill-ponds, and fences; Surveyor, again with large authority, of walls, ditches, gutters, sewers, bridges, causeways, et cetera, along the Thames between Greenwich and Woolwich; Clerk of the Works at Windsor; Sub-Forester, and later Forester, in control of the great royal forest domain of Petherton in Somerset; and in the intervals holder of important ward-ships, and associated in the management of great estates. And finally, not to omit the element of adventure, it may be doubted if there was ever another English poet who was twice robbed by highwaymen within three days. I have crammed into a catalogue, for the sake of their cumulative impact, the facts which everybody knows, but which we habitually contemplate piecemeal. And the active search still going on in the Records Office is bringing to light from time to time new items which further diversify the list. Had Chaucer never written a line of poetry, he would still have been known to his contemporaries as a trusted and capable public servant and a many-sided man of affairs.

What that rich experience meant for his art is for us the essential thing. But what it might have meant to it and by the grace of Heaven did not, it is neither irrelevant nor uninstructive to observe. Chaucer's French contemporary, Eustache Deschamps, who sent him a famous poetical epistle and who will meet us later, also led an active and a semi-public life, and into his twelve hundred *balades*, his one hundred and seventy-one *rondeaux*, his eighteen *virelais*, his fifteen *lais*, which nobody ever reads any more except as documents, he poured on occasion the minute and personal details of his variegated career—dates and places meticu-lously noted; incidents of his campaigns in Flanders; the

racy interchange of bilingual amenities with two English-
men as he and Othon de Graunson (Chaucer's 'flour of
hem that make in Fraunce') one day rode through Calais;
the fleas at the inn that night; his personal ailments; his
distaste for tripe and truffles. Now Chaucer had at his
fingers' ends more such themes for verse than ever Deschamps dreamed. Read sometime, for its equally sinister
possibilities, the inventory in the *Life Records* which Chaucer
turned in when he resigned the Clerkship of the Works—
pages on pages of rakes, ladles, crowbars, hurdles for
scaffolds—one remembers how 'joly Absalon', the parish
clerk, played Herod 'on a scaffold hye'—, andirons in-
numerable, a broken cable ('frangitur et devastatur'),
images made in the likeness of kings, '100 round stones
called engynstones', bottles, buckets, and (from the Tower
of London of all places) a frying-pan. And there were also
the sewers and the gutters and the ditches. What use
Deschamps would have made of such opportunities does
not admit of contemplation. But only once that I can recall
in the whole wide range of his poetry does Chaucer give
even a hint of his participation in affairs. It was in another
and a different fashion that his extraordinarily varied experience played into the hands of his art. And if in what
follows I may seem for a time to have wholly forgotten that
art, I can only ask you to believe that I have not.

What that experience gave to Chaucer was, of course,
first of all an opportunity almost unrivalled for wide and
intimate knowledge of almost every sort of actor in the
human comedy. We are apt to forget in thinking of him
the remarkable range of his acquaintance with men and
women in virtually every station, rank, and occupation of
the diversified society in which he lived. He was a member
of the household, first of a prince of the blood and then of a
king, and through his marriage belonged to the circle of
John of Gaunt and Henry of Derby. He counted among his
acquaintances and friends great nobles and knights who had
travelled far, and fought in all quarters of the known world.

On his missions abroad he was associated with men of wide experience and influence in State affairs; met in France and Flanders statesmen versed in diplomacy; and matched his wits in Italy with Bernabò Visconti—'God of delyt, and scourge of Lumbardye', as he called him when the message reached him of his sudden end. The very first record that we have of him contains a reference to a visit of Prince Lionel and the Countess of Ulster, on whom he was then in attendance, to the Benedictine Nunnery of St. Leonards, at the Prioress's Stratford atte Bowe, and from then to the close of his life he had intimate knowledge in a score of ways—through members of his own family, connexions by marriage, and the infinite ramifications of the Church's influence upon affairs—of ecclesiastics of every feather. With men of law he came, through various exigencies, into close relations, and there is reason to think that he may himself have been a member of Lincoln's Inn. He had business dealings for years with merchants and shipmen, and through his Clerkships of the Works and his Surveyor-ships, with masons and carpenters and hedgers and ditchers and unskilled labour of every sort. And how closely his relations with the tradesmen and the craftsmen of the guilds were bound up with his own political career, Professor Kuhl years ago made clear. Now and then one gets a glimpse of that rare and precious thing a concrete incident, as when one sees him (in that record which Miss Rickert turned up a year or so ago) going down from the Customs to Dart-mouth about a Genoese tarit, the 'Saint Mary and Saint George'—its master one Johannes de Nigris of Genoa—which had been driven ashore on the coast of Brittany, and which John Hawley, then Mayor of Dartmouth, was charged with robbing. And one of Hawley's ships was called the 'Maude-layne', and Chaucer had the trick of turning official business to good poetic account. There are still vast uncharted regions of the Public Records to explore, but Professor Manly's recent studies of them have given as never before —whether or not we grant this or that tentative conclusion

—flesh and blood and sometimes local habitation to the sergeants of law, the merchants, franklins and shipmen, the millers and weavers, the archdeacons, canons, summoners, friars, pardoners, prioresses and nuns, whom Chaucer first knew for his day and then bequeathed to eternity.

But this wide range of his experience carries with it another consequence. We need constantly to remind ourselves of the degree to which in Chaucer's day communication had to be by word of mouth. And so the people whom he knew were also channels through which came to him news of his world—news not only of that 'little world' which to Shakespeare's John of Gaunt was England; not only, either, of that 'queasy world' (in Margaret Paston's vivid phrase) across the Channel; but also of that now looming, menacing, always mysterious world beyond, which was the Orient. And few men have ever been more strategically placed for its reception. That news of England or Wales or even Ireland should so reach him is too obvious to dwell on, fascinating as is the use he makes of it. How, for example, did he get to know of that 'Colle tregetour'—Colin the magician —whom he saw in his dream in the House of Fame?

> Ther saugh I Colle tregetour
> Upon a table of sicamour
> Pleye an uncouthe thing to telle;
> I saugh him carien a wind-melle
> Under a walsh-note shelle.

But Colle was actually no piquant figure in a dream. He was, as we now know, thanks to Professor Royster, a contemporary Englishman, and he later exhibited his tricks, 'par voie de nigromancie', at Orleans, precisely as the Clerk of Orleans in the Franklin's Tale produced his illusions, 'Swiche as thise subtile tregetoures playe'. And Chaucer's apposite choice of Orleans as the school of his own magician is not without interest. How, too (to draw on the House of Fame again), did he get to know of Bret Glascurion and of Celtic wicker houses? Did that Welsh vintner of London tell him—Lewis Johan, who was at least a friend of Chaucer once removed; or did Sir Lewis Clifford or Sir John Clanvowe, both close friends of his, and both of whom held offices in Wales? Who can say! Chaucer's London was his own vast House of Rumour, only on a smaller scale.

But men, among them scores whom Chaucer knew, were constantly going out of England and coming back to it— going out for reasons of war, or trade, or chivalry, or religion, and coming back along the trade routes and the pilgrim roads and from their military exploits, with stories, and tidings, and even manuscripts, as well as with stuffs, or spices, or cockle-shells, or battered arms. And such knights as the stately figure of the Prologue were among the great intermediaries between Chaucer's England and the rest of the world. Europe was being menaced from three directions at once. We sometimes forget that Tamerlane's life just overlapped Chaucer's at each end, and that it was in the year in which Chaucer was appointed Justice of the Peace that the Great Turk boasted that he would make his horse eat oats on the high altar of St. Peter's. And Chaucer's Knight had fought in Europe, Asia, and Africa against the Moors, the Turks, the Tartars and the heathen of the North—in Turkey, Spain, Prussia, Lithuania (then a Tartar outpost) and Russia, and also with 'that valorous champion of impossible conquests', Pierre de Lusignan, King of Cyprus, at the taking of Alexandria, and at Lyeys and Satalye. And the knight was a composite portrait of men whom Chaucer personally knew. Of the witnesses (to give a single instance) who testified with Chaucer in the Scrope-Grosvenor case, Nicholas Sambraham, Esquire, had seen Sir Stephen Scrope at the taking of Alexandria, and in Hungary, Prussia, and Constantinople, and had seen Sir Henry Scrope in Spain, and, as he says, 'beyond the great sea in many places and in many chivalrous exploits'. Sir Richard Waldegrave had seen Sir William Scrope with the King of Cyprus at Satalye in Turkey; and Sir Henry de Ferrers and John de Ri her, Esquire, had seen Sir Geoffrey Scrope in Prussia and Lithuania. And these half-dozen names we know through the accident of a dispute about the bearing of certain arms. There are more, but these are enough to show that the campaigns of Chaucer's Knight were the campaigns of Chaucer's acquaintances and friends. And they, like the Knight, had been associated with fellow knights of all the other nations which, with England, were making common cause against a common foe. And such stories as circulated about those Tables of Honour, like that at the head of which the Knight had often sat 'aboven alle naciouns in Pruce', and tales of that gallant and meteoric figure, the King of Cyprus, whose death Chaucer bewailed 'in maner of Tragedie', and of tournaments at Tramissene and sea-fights off the coasts of Africa and Asia Minor—such stories a score of Chaucer's friends could tell. For warfare was a more leisured business then than now—witness the Barbary expedition, of which Chaucer's friends Sir Lewis Clifford and Sir John Clanvowe were members, during which warlike expedition the gay and amorous *Cent Balades* were composed. And finally—to come closer home —it was to a meeting in France, during a pause in the Hundred Years' War, between this same friend Sir Lewis Clifford and Eustache Deschamps, that there came to Chaucer the manuscript which suggested his best-known passage outside the Canterbury Tales; as it was through a later meeting between the same two men, during the negotiations for a truce, that Chaucer received another manuscript which gave him rich material for the most famous portrait in the Tales themselves.

Chivalry, too, played its curious part. Don Quixote, Professor Ker once observed with chapter and verse, would have been perfectly at home with the Knights and Squires of Chaucer's day, and would not have been thought extravagant in either principles or practice. And with that dictum no student of the period will disagree. And so young Squires who, like Machaut's and Chaucer's, bore them well in arms 'in hope to stonden in [hir] lady grace', were still being sent by their ladies to win further grace,

'in-to Walakye, To Pruyse and in-to Tartarye, To Ali-
saundre, ne in-to Turkye', and finally charged, for the
crowning exploit, to 'Go hoodles to the drye see, And come
hoom by the Carrenar'. And that last injunction is a
singularly apposite case in point. For we now know, as
Sir Aurel Stein's latest maps and photographs at last
unmistakably show, that an actual Kara-nor, or Black Lake,
lies a short stone's throw from Marco Polo's highway, in the
heart of Central Asia, beyond the dry, salt-incrusted bed of
an ancient inland sea. And through some merchant or
other this bit of flotsam and jetsam had probably drifted
back along the silk routes, perhaps through Lyeys, where
the Knight had fought, along with who can tell what tales
of Tartary, such as that which the Squire himself was to
rehearse.

For merchants, with pilgrims and shipmen, were also
recognized bearers of news, and as such Chaucer, on whose
own testimony I am drawing, knew them well. 'Ye ben
fadres of tydinges And tales,' exclaims the Man of Law in his
apostrophe to merchants; 'Tydings of sondry regnes' he
goes on, and of 'the wondres that they mighte seen or here'.
And it was a merchant, he declares, who years ago told him
the very tale he tells—a story which begins in Syria and
wanders by way of the Pillars of Hercules to England, and
back by the strait to Italy. For England, like all of Europe,
was full of tales—tales which through centuries had travelled
by mysterious routes from Arabia and Hindostan and
Burma and Tibet and Turkey and Siberia—narratives
ageless and timeless, with no abiding place; rubbed smooth
in their endless passings, like pebbles rounded by the waves,
or Chinese carvings polished by uncounted generations of
hands. Nor was it only merchants along the trade routes who
were their vehicles. Chaucer's House of Rumour 'Was ful
of shipmen and pilgrymes, With scrippes bret-ful of lesinges,
Entremedled with tydinges'. And pilgrims like that notable
wayfarer the Wife of Bath, who had thrice been at Jerusalem,
and 'had passed many a straunge streem', were visiting

'ferne halwes, couthe in sondry londes', and coming back, like the merchants, with multifarious information, false and true. It was along the pilgrim roads, as we now well know, that the stories of Charlemagne and Roland and the twelve peers of France passed over the Alps into Italy. And pilgrims told their tales, and Chaucer was a marvellous listener. His Dartmouth shipman, too, whose own harbour was one of the English ports for ships from the Orient, knew 'alle the havenes, as they were, From Gootlond to the cape of Finistere, And every cryke in Britayne and in Spayne'. And Gothland, with the other havens at which he and his fellows touched, was connected through the Hanseatic trade with Novgorod, and Novgorod, like the ports in Asia Minor where Chaucer's friends had fought, had been for hundreds of years a terminus of those ancient Eastern trade-routes along which had travelled, with the merchants and the shipmen, tales like those which underlie the *fabliaux* and a dozen of the stories which the Canterbury pilgrims tell. And Chaucer sat at the receipt of custom in the port of London, 'at the quay called Wool-wharf in the Tower Ward'. And the man who, between nightfall and bedtime, had spoken with every one of the nine and twenty pilgrims at the Tabard Inn was not the man to refrain from incidental conversation with the mariners whose lawful occasions brought them to his quay.

How this or that particular tale or bit of information came to Chaucer, it is far from my present purpose to inquire. He was at the centre of a rich and varied and shifting world, and in ways without number, of which these are bare suggestions, his personal and official experience lent material to his art. And there were also books.

The range of Chaucer's reading is as extraordinary as the scope of his activities. He read in three languages besides English—French, Latin, and Italian. French he probably both knew and spoke from his childhood. Latin with little doubt he learned at school. It has hitherto been assumed that he picked up Italian in Italy, during his first visit in

1372-3. It is possible, though not yet proven, that he may have known it earlier. But in either case, the bulk of his known reading, until the great Italians swam into his ken, was French, with a good deal of Latin besides. And French he never abandoned, and Latin he read copiously to the end. The French and Italian works which he knew may best for our purpose be considered later. His wide and diversified reading of Latin, however, is both typical of his varied interests and important for its contributions, and I shall rapidly summarize it here.

Of the classics he knew in the original Ovid, especially the *Metamorphoses* (his 'owne book', as he called it), and the *Heroides*. Virgil he knew, but apparently only the *Aeneid*; the *Thebaid* of Statius; Claudian; and either in Latin or French or both, the *Pharsalia*. Cicero's *Somnium Scipionis* he read in a copy of the commentary of Macrobius which he or somebody else had thumbed to pieces—'myn olde book to-torn', as he refers to it. Horace he quotes half a dozen times, but I doubt whether he knew either Horace or Juvenal at first hand. Dante, or John of Salisbury, or the *florilegia* may well have been intermediaries. But for Virgil, Statius, and Lucan, and also for Ovid, he had two strings to his bow. For the Middle Ages seized upon the Latin epics and made them over into their own likeness as romances. And so there was, for the *Aeneid*, the *Roman d'Eneas*, in which both Dido and (especially) Lavinia sigh, wake, and 'walwe', like Chaucer's own Dido in the *Legend*, in the throes of heroic love. For the *Thebaid*, too, there was the *Roman de Thèbes*, and for the *Pharsalia* the *Roman de Julius Cesar*. And the Homeric story of the Trojan War passed by devious ways into the *Roman de Troie* of Benoit de Ste-Maure, and thence to Guido delle Colonne. The *Metamorphoses* were transmogrified into the interminable and portentous triple allegory of the *Ovide moralisé*, on which Machaut had freely drawn for his classical lore. They are all, as I can testify, diverting documents, after their fantastic fashion, even yet, and Chaucer, who probably in his salad days read French more readily than Latin, and who also would be apt to read what his fellow pages and squires at Court were reading, certainly knew and freely used the *Roman de Troie*, and drew, on occasion, upon the *Ovide moralisé*. He also read—I feel sure myself on grounds which have no place here—the *Roman d'Eneas* and the *Roman de Julius Cesar*. And there is evidence that he knew the mythographers, and was not unfamiliar with the mass of misinformation accumulated in the medieval commentaries on the classics. It was, in fact, more than once Servius or Lactantius or Junius Philargerius who either directly or indirectly first made for him his mistakes. For few things about Chaucer are more important to remember than the fact that even the classical authors whom he read in the original were deeply coloured in his mind through the various medieval metamorphoses which they had undergone.

His reading in the medieval Latin authors was far too extensive for enumeration here. But nothing in his dealings with them is more characteristic than his trick of suffusing with his own inalienable humour his borrowings from the dullest and most arid documents. He knew well both the *Anticlaudianus* and the *De Planctu Naturae* of Alanus de Insulis, and especially remembered, as he would, the concrete bits, and enriched them, as he also would, with an added liveliness. He read Martianus Capella on the Nuptials of Philology and Mercury, and Nigel Wireker's diverting Mirror of Fools, with the adventures of Dan Burnel the ass; and a scrap of the Eclogue of Theodulus once leaped back to his memory, endowed with an exquisite humour which he did not find in his original. He knew, as a student of his art, who did not 'pipe but as the linnets sing', the *Nova Poetria* of Geoffrey of Vinsauf, whom he calls his 'dere mayster soverayn', and he made irresistible mock-heroic use, in the Nuns' Priest's Tale, of one of his master's *exempla*. He at least dipped into the vast encyclopaedic reaches of Vincent of Beauvais, and he read with obvious gusto and astounding results St. Jerome's tractate against Jovinian on the subject of virginity. He was thoroughly familiar (to shift the key) with the Vulgate, and with the service and especially the great hymns of the Church, which inspired —in each case interwoven with lines from the crowning vision of the *Paradiso*—at least two of his loftiest passages. Whether he saw as he read the rich potentialities of his documents, or whether his stores came pouring back to memory as he composed, or whether both processes went on together, we can never know. But if any one ever read (in the current phrase) 'creatively', it was he.

And to all this evidence of abounding vitality and energy must be added the almost incredible list of his translations. The refrain of the *Balade* which Eustache Deschamps addressed to Chaucer and sent by the hand of Sir Lewis Clifford, is the line: 'Grant translateur, noble Geffroy Chaucier.' It was as a translator only, it would seem, that his fame had reached Deschamps. And the *Balade* itself makes it clear that Deschamps had in mind that translation of the *Roman de la Rose* which, in the Prologue to the *Legend*, gave such offence to the God of Love. And the God of Love's anger makes it further clear that Jean de Meun's huge continuation was included. As if this great task were not enough, he translated Jean de Meun's French version of Albertano of Brescia's *Liber Consolationis*, and also (for his tastes were richly catholic) the fierce misanthropy of Pope Innocent's *De Contemptu Mundi*, at which gloomy treatise Deschamps too had tried his hand. And there were besides the now lost translations of a work of Origen on Mary Magdalene, and of Machaut's *Dit dou Lyon*. But above all the rest stands Boethius *On the Consolation of Philosophy*. He translated it, as Alfred the Great and Jean de Meun had done before him, and with the aid of Jean de Meun's French version, and he drew upon it, as in another fashion he levied tribute on the *Roman de la Rose*, until he ceased to write.

His reading in the science of his day is in some respects, I am inclined to think, the most remarkable of all. His singularly broad yet minute knowledge of medieval medicine, in which he anticipated Burton, I have elsewhere had occasion to discuss. But far more than his acquaintance with 'the loveres maladye of Hereos' is in point. Fourteenth-century medicine, like its twentieth-century descendant, was half psychology, and in its emphasis on dreams as a means of diagnosis anticipated Freud. And Madame Pertelote's diagnosis, by means of his dream, of Chauntecleer's malady, as well as her inimitable discourse on dreams as symptoms, is scientifically accurate. So is her *materia medica*. The herbs which she prescribes—'Pekke hem up right as they growe, and ete hem in'—are the medically proper herbs. And the quintessential touch is her inclusion in Chauntecleer's dietary of 'wormes' for 'a day or two'. For worms—you may read a learned and matter-of-fact chapter on *Vermes terrenae* in the *Medica Materia* of Dioscorides—were among the recognized correctives. It is easy enough to slip into one's narrative as evidence of erudition an excerpt from some learned document. But such casual exactness, imbued with delicious humour to boot, is not something which one gets up over night. In alchemy—witness the Canon's Yeoman's Tale—Chaucer was no less deeply grounded than in medicine. He had read enough in the alchemical treatises of Arnoldus de Villanova, for example, his 'Arnold of the Newe Toun', to refer to one of Arnold's treatises a highly picturesque and abstruse dictum which he quotes, when he had actually read it in another. As for physics, one of the very best pieces of exposition, as exposition, which I know in English is the erudite Eagle's discourse in the House of Fame on the transmission of sound, and that again is founded on accepted authority. So is Chaucer's astrology, and in astronomy proper he could point with just pride to that Treatise on the Astrolabe which he wrote, with its charming Preface, for his 'litel son Lowis', using freely a Latin translation of the Arabian astronomer Messahala. These are the barest shreds and patches only. The scope and thoroughness of Chaucer's scientific reading would still be remarkable, had he read nothing else.

There, then, are the raw materials of his art—men and their doings, and books—God's plenty of each, in all conscience. And since he began with books (with which, to be sure, he never ended) it is much to the point to consider how he read. Did he have the books on our list, for example, in his own possession, and therefore ready at hand for pleasure or need? Without question a large, perhaps a very large proportion of them were his own. He declared, fairly late in his life—or rather, the God of Love asserted for him —that he had in his chest 'sixty bokes, olde and newe', and there is no reason to doubt the statement. But that number may easily have represented three or four times sixty 'books', in the sense in which we use the word. For book, as Chaucer employs the term, must be thought of in the light of medieval manuscripts, and a single manuscript was often a small library in itself. The 'boke' which Chaucer was reading when he fell asleep over the tale of Ceyx and Alcyone was an omnium gatherum of verse, and lives of queens and kings, and 'many othere thinges smale'. The 'book' (and again the word is the same) which the Wife of Bath's fifth husband revelled in contained, she declared, Valerius *ad Rufinum*, Theophrastus, Jerome against Jovinian, Tertullian, the mysterious Crisippus, Trotula, the Epistles of Eloise, the Parables of Solomon, and the *Ars Amatoria*—'And alle thise were bounden in o volume'. And one need only recall, among extant examples, the Auchinleck MS., with its more than forty separate pieces, or, for that matter, Harley 7333 among the manuscripts of the Canterbury Tales. Chaucer's library was a rich one for his day, and like his own clerk of Oxford who had 'at his beddes heed' his 'Twenty bokes, clad in blak or reed', and like that clerk of another kidney, 'hende Nicholas', who likewise kept in his lodgings 'his Almageste, and bokes grete and smale ... On shelves couched at his beddes heed', one may be fairly sure that Chaucer's sixty books were not far from his hand.

But is there any way of knowing, aside from these more or less material considerations, how he actually read? There are two subjects, and two only, on which Chaucer vouchsafes us personal information about himself—his love of books, and his imperviousness, real or assumed, to love. On those two topics he is, in William Wordsworth's phrase but with a difference, 'right voluble'. And two passages are especially in point. In one, that preternaturally intelligent bird, the Eagle of the House of Fame, gently chides him for his habits. He knows nothing now, says the Eagle, of what is going on about him; even 'of thy verray neyghebores That dwellen almost at thy dores, Thou herest neither that ne this'. And then follows, under cover of the Eagle's irresponsible loquacity, the most precious autobiographical touch that Chaucer left:

> For whan thy labour doon al is,
> And hast y-maad thy rekeninges,
> In stede of reste and newe thinges,
> Thou gost hoom to thy hous anoon;
> And, also domb as any stoon,
> Thou sittest at another boke,
> Til fully daswed is thy loke,
> And livest thus as an hermyte,
> Although thyn abstinence is lyte.

That picture—the account books of the customs exchanged after hours for vastly different books (the Eagle's 'another' is pregnant), and Chaucer reading on, oblivious of all else, until his eyes dazzle in his head—that picture tells more than pages, not merely of the intimate relation in which his books stood to his business, but also of the absorbed intentness with which he read. And there is another passage which illuminates yet another quality of his reading. 'Not yore agon', he writes in the Parlement of Foules,

> . . . hit happed me for to beholde
> Upon a boke, was write with lettres olde;
> And ther-upon, *a certeyn thing to lerne*,
> The longe day *ful faste I radde and yerne*.

I do not know which is the more characteristic of Chaucer—

the fact that he was reading with the definite purpose of learning a certain thing, or the fact that he was reading fast and eagerly. The two belong together. You cannot divide his invincible zest from his incorrigibly inquiring spirit— that 'besy gost' of his, as he called it once, 'that thrusteth alwey newe'. And because he brought both to his books, his reading became a live and plastic thing for his art to seize on.

He was gifted, finally, with another quality of mind which is peculiarly bound up with his art. He possessed, in a word, like Virgil and Milton and Coleridge, a powerfully associative memory, which played, as he read, over the multitude of impressions from previous reading, with which his mind was stored. And the zest with which he read gave freshness to his recollections, and one can sometimes almost see the hovering associations precipitate themselves as he reads. A single phrase in Boccaccio (and I am speaking by the book) calls up the lines of a famous passage in Dante in which the same phrase occurs, and the result is a *tertium quid* of his own, enriched from the spoils of both. He finds in Boccaccio's *Filostrato*, as he works it over into his own Troilus, the lovely Virgilian simile of the lily cut by the plough and withering. But Dante, in a canto of the *Inferno*, the opening lines of which Chaucer elsewhere quotes, has a simile of falling, withering leaves. And again, through a common element, Boccaccio's lines recall the lines of Dante, and the falling leaves replace the fading lily in Chaucer's simile. And Boccaccio and Dante in turn had each in like fashion recalled his simile from Virgil. It would be easy to rehearse such instances by the score—instances, too, in which with his reminiscences of books are interwoven his recollections of experience. For that continuity of poetry of which I spoke consists in the perpetual enrichment, through just such incremental transformations, of the present through the past. And one of the happiest gifts of the gods to English poetry, at the strategic moment of its history, was that prehensile, amalgamating memory of Chaucer's which had for its playground the prodigious array of promiscuous writings which a moment ago I ruthlessly catalogued.

What now of his art in its larger relations? For everything that I have so far said has been said with that definitely in view. It is perilous, in the first place, to divide Chaucer's poetic biography mechanically into periods. There was nothing cataclysmic about his development. He was not a new creature, as Professor Kittredge once observed, when he came back to London from his first visit to Italy, nor does the poet of the Canterbury Tales startle us by a 'leap of buds into ripe flowers'. Rather—if I too may yield to an association—'Morn into noon did pass, noon into eve'. Transitions there were, of course, but they were gradual. French poetry yielded first place to Italian, and both to an absorption in human life, in which books and men were fused as in a crucible. But even after his momentous discovery of Boccaccio and Dante, the influence of French poetry went on, though its character changed—changed (to put it briefly) from the mood of Guillaume de Lorris and Machaut to the mood of Jean de Meun and Deschamps and the *fabliaux*. And *pari passu*, as his powers developed, there came a significant shift of values, and his reading of books played a lesser and his reading of life a larger role in his art. But throughout his career, that art kept curiously even pace with his active life. It was dominantly French while he was in personal attendance on a court where French was still the more familiar language. His so-called Italian period, which was never Italian in the sense in which the earlier period had been French, coincided roughly with those activities—his missions and the customs—which brought him into various relations with Italy, Italians, and Italian letters. And when his broadening affairs afforded wider opportunities for observation, his art, keeping all that it had won from France and Italy, became at once English and universal.

Everybody knows that Chaucer began as a follower of the contemporary French school of poetry, and that the most powerful influence upon that school was the thirteenth-century *Roman de la Rose*. But the *Roman de la Rose* was influential in two entirely different ways. Guillaume de Lorris, who began it, was a dreamer of dreams and a poet of exquisite grace and charm. Jean de Meun, who continued it and multiplied its length by five, was a caustic and disillusioned satirist, trenchant, arrogant, and absolute master of a mordant pen. If Pope had taken it into his head to complete the *Faerie Queene*, or if Swift had been seized by the fancy of carrying on the *Vicar of Wakefield* in the mood of Gulliver's fierce misanthropy, we might have had an adequate parallel. And the fourteenth-century French poets, as a consequence of this strange duplex authorship, fall roughly into two schools—the sons of Guillaume de Lorris and the sons of Jean de Meun. But common to them all, and giving the framework to half their verse, was the allegorical love vision.

The contemporary Frenchmen whose influence on Chaucer was farthest reaching were three: Guillaume de Machaut, an elder contemporary; Jean Froissart, his coeval; and Eustache Deschamps, who was younger. Machaut, who like Chaucer was courtier and man of affairs as well as poet, and who with his master, John of Bohemia, had 'reysed', like the Knight, against the 'mescreans' in Prussia and the Tartars in the snows of Lithuania, was the most influential French poet of his day. And he was so chiefly by virtue of a highly sophisticated, artificial, exquisitely elaborated technique. Froissart, whom Chaucer probably knew at Court as the protégé of Queen Philippa, was an incomparably less finished craftsman than Machaut, to whose school he belongs. When he tells a story, like that in the *Dit dou Florin*, of his reading aloud to Gaston Phebus, Count of Foix, night after night for weeks, his interminable *Méliador*, the tale becomes, through the art of the chronicler, vivid with firelight and candles and flagons; and when he writes of his boyhood and young manhood—of the games that he played, and of the maiden whom he one day found reading the *Cléomadès*—his verse is suffused with personal charm. But when he falls into the vein of the school, he can be both long-winded and very dull. And finally Deschamps, who calls Machaut his master, but who was really of the tribe of Jean de Meun, was an inordinately prolific versifier, with the skill of a virtuoso, but without music, grace, or charm; could be as minutely circumstantial as Mistress Quickly over her silver-gilt goblet; and was possessed by a passion like that of Pepys for autobiographical memoranda. Of the three, Machaut was Chaucer's earliest master; from Froissart he effectively borrowed more than once; and Deschamps twice furnished him with subject matter to which, on the two occasions, each time with a technique already mastered, he gave consummate form. There were others, of course, but these three were the chief influences during the period when Chaucer was saturated with the later French poetry of courtly love, even while maintaining an amiable impermeability all his own to its inherent absurdities. And I am far from sure that it was not to these very absurdities that Chaucer's genius owed the turn which from the first it took.

For he found in his French models, and especially in Machaut, the framework of the vision, as that had come down, with growing elaboration on the way, from Guillaume de Lorris. And he used the machinery of the vision in the Book of the Duchess, the House of Fame, the Parliament of Fowls, and in the first version of the Prologue to the Legend of Good Women. It was the most popular and, in Machaut's expert hands, the most sophisticated device of his day, and Chaucer was then writing for a sophisticated audience. But the visions were allegorical love visions, and as such they were thick sown with artifices at which Chaucer balked. And the more thoroughly one is steeped in Chaucer, so that one sees in a measure with his eyes, the more readily one understands the impossibility of his acquiescence in the then current artificialities of the *genre*. The framework of the vision, to be sure, offered freedom in both choice and disposition of subject matter. But it was precisely in the character of the French subject matter, to judge from the cold shoulder which Chaucer turned to it, that one source of his disrelish lay. For it was obviously as barren of interest to Geoffrey Chaucer as interminable subtilizings about love—especially when nothing comes of them—have been and are to any normally constituted Anglo-Saxon. Moreover, the visions are thickly peopled with personified abstractions. Esperance, Attemprance, Mesure, Douce Pensée, Plaisance, Desirs, Franchise, Pité, Loyauté, Espoirs, Raison, Suffisance, Patience, Paour—those are the denizens of less than half of Machaut's *Remede de Fortune*. Like Criseyde listening under trying circumstances to the 'wommanisshe thinges' of her feminine callers, Chaucer must have 'felte almost [his] herte dye For wo, and wery of that companye'. Nor was it subject matter alone which he found alien. The phraseology, too, was remote alike from his tastes and his aptitudes. There is nothing I know which rivals in its tireless facility of recurrence the later vocabulary of courtly love. If one read long enough, one is obsessed by the uncanny feeling that the phraseology walks alone, without need of the poet's intervention, and carries the poet with it of its own momentum. Specific meaning disappears. Machaut's Peronne, in that amazing Goethe-and-Bettina correspondence, the *Voir-Dit*, is 'en douceur douce com coulombelle, En loyauté loyal com turturelle'. But the same columbine phrases slip from his pen, when, in *Prise d'Alexandrie*, he describes the Emperor Charles I of Luxembourg. He too, like Peronne, is 'humbles et piteus Plus que turtre ne colombele'. In that ineffably affected jargon discriminations vanish. 'Thought and affliction, passion, hell itself, [are turned] to favour and to prettiness.' And that was not Chaucer's way.

What he found, then, in the French vision poems, was a *frame*—a frame which possessed admirable potentialities, but which for him, to all intents and purposes, was empty. And Chaucer, who in his way was not unlike Nature herself, abhorred a vacuum. He proceeded, accordingly, to fill the frame, and incidentally to set one of the great traditions of English poetry. And into the vision framework, instead of consecrated phrases, wire-drawn subtleties, *ragiona-mente d'amore*, and the more fantastic elements of the courtly code, he poured the stores of that reading and observation on which we have dwelt so long. 'For out of olde feldes'— and this was his discovery, as 'the longe day ful faste [he] radde and yerne'—

> For out of olde feldes, as man seith,
> Cometh al this newe corn fro yeer to yere;
> And out of olde bokes, in good feith,
> Cometh al this newe science that men lere.

And into the old bottles Chaucer poured with lavish hand a new and heady wine.

What happened may best be seen by a glance at his first three vision poems. His earliest essay, the Book of the Duchess, was made before he went to Italy, when his reading was almost wholly French, and when Machaut in particular was at his finger tips. It is a vision poem, with all the paraphernalia of the *genre*, and it is also an elegy—an elegy on the death of the Duchess Blanche, the first wife of his patron, John of Gaunt. But into the conventional frame he fits, with tact and feeling, and with conspicuous skill in adapting them to his ends, materials drawn from what was then his reading—to wit, in this instance, from no less than eight of Machaut's poems and one (at least) of Froissart's. Save for scattered reminiscences of the Bible, the *Roman de la Rose*, Boethius, and Benoit, there is little else. His instinct from the beginning was to enrich, and those were the stores which he then possessed. But his borrowings are interwoven with such art that for more than five hundred years nobody suspected that the poem was not all of a piece. And even when his appropriations are most unmistakable, they are still miraculously Chaucer and not Machaut. The little whelp that came creeping up, as if it knew him, to the Dreamer, and 'Hild doun his heed and joyned his eres, And leyde al smothe doun his heres'—that bewitching English puppy is Chaucer's metamorphosis of a fantastic lion, which Carpaccio would have revelled in, native to the bizarre landscape of the *Dit dou Lyon* of Machaut. And into his version of Machaut's catalogue of those remote regions to which the courtly lovers were dispatched to win their spurs, Chaucer has slipped that precious bit of hearsay about the Dry Sea and the Carrenar. The Book of the Duchess is not a masterpiece, but it is significant far beyond its intrinsic merit. For in it for the first time, with the still limited resources at his command, Chaucer loaded every rift with ore. And now the ore grew steadily richer.

For Chaucer went to Italy, and learned to read Boccaccio and Dante, and all the while that knowledge of books and men on which we have dwelt was broadening and deepening. The French influence waned as that of Italy waxed, but the shift of emphasis was gradual, and the vision poems still went on. And into the three that followed the Book of the Duchess poured those steadily growing stores. He begins the House of Fame—to follow what seems to me to be the true succession—a little dully, with a long résumé of the *Aeneid*, and an interlude from the *Metamorphoses*. And both the *Roman d'Eneas* and the *Ovide moralisé* were summoned, I feel certain, to his aid. Then all at once, into a desert recalled from Lucan sweeps an eagle which owed its sunlike brightness to the *Paradiso*, and the poem becomes vivid with new life. And the significant thing is not so much that the amazing eagle, throughout the flight through the air, shows himself equally at home in Ovid, and Boethius, and Theodulus, and Macrobius, and Dante's *Convito*, and can even recognize Chaucer's unspoken thoughts of Martianus Capella and Alanus, as that he is a new and unique creation —as much a person as his creator, and utterly unthinkable in any vision which Machaut and his fellows ever dreamed. And only the keenest observer of men, endowed with the rarest humour, could have conceived the inimitable conversation which goes on, as the little earth recedes to a speck and the signs of the zodiac are left behind; and the poet of the Canterbury Tales is already present in that immortal dialogue. Then, into the third book, ushered in, like the second, by an invocation drawn from Dante, pours a phantasmagoria which Rabelais might have envied, and which defies all summary—reminiscences of books treading on the heels of recollections of experience, in bewildering profusion. Within the compass of thirty-five lines—to take a relatively simple passage only—Chaucer's memory, as the verse flows on without a ripple, has flashed to Boethius, and the *Roman de la Rose*, and a line from the *Metamorphoses*, and some account or other which he had read in the romances of those whirling houses which were a peculiarly captivating item in the romantic stock-in-trade, and Celtic wicker houses which he had either seen himself or heard of from his friends, and the noise of 'engynstones' remembered from his own campaign in France. Sketched as I am sketching it, the poem is a thing of shreds and patches. It is not so on the page. But I am putting asunder what Chaucer joined together, in order to give the barest inkling of the thronging recollections which, in his vision poems, his art curbed and concealed.

And now, in the Parlement of Foules, France slips gradually into the background and Italy assumes the major role. The cadre of the vision is still retained, but the familiar French couplet is discarded, and rime royal takes its place. In the last two books of the House of Fame Chaucer's crowding recollections are swept along as by a torrent; in the close-packed introductory sections of the Parlement there is a new serenity, and a sense of beauty which has been quickened and deepened alike. For the influence of Dante and Boccaccio upon Chaucer is to be sought not merely or even chiefly in his borrowings and imitations, but rather through the impregnation of his art with qualities which his earlier French masters never knew. And in the first half of the Parlement Chaucer's memory is busy with the Divine Comedy, and both his memory and his eyes with the *Teseide*. The Proem opens with a rendering, in a master's hand, of the first axiom of Hippocrates—

> The lyf so short, the craft so long to lerne,
> Th'assay so hard, so sharp the conquering.

It was a favourite with those elder medical authorities whom Chaucer read, and I suspect it came to him from them. Then, passing to the book which he had just been reading 'faste and yerne' all day long, he gives (I am sure for his own delight) a summary—compact and lucid and urbane—of the *Somnium Scipionis*. And night falls in the words with which Dante describes the first fall of evening in the *Inferno*. Then Chaucer's unrest before he sleeps recalls Boethius, and the thought of dreams brings back to mind the famous lines of Claudian, and because (as Chaucer shrewdly suggests) he has just been reading the dream of Scipio, Scipio himself becomes his guide. And the Proem ends with a flash of memory back to Jean de Meun.

Of the next one hundred lines or so, Boccaccio's *Teseide*, through a score of its most graphic and beautiful stanzas, has the lion's share. Twice at least, too, a phrase of Boccaccio recalls a passage of Dante, and the *Divina Commedia* and the *Teseide* flow together into a mould which is Chaucer's own. And *Inferno*, *Purgatorio*, and *Paradiso* are now all three at command. Then all at once the whole character of the vision changes. From the robe of the 'noble emperesse' Nature in Aleyn's 'Pleynt of Kinde', Chaucer sweeps the birds of the air which Alanus had depicted on it, adds others of his own, and sets them down before Nature, alive and gifted with the power of speech, in parliament assembled. And whatever, if any, the ulterior purpose of the poem, that assembly, with its unerring adjustment of sentiments and language to the ranks and classes of the fowls, was conceived and executed by a keen and detached observer of the foibles, not of worm-fowls, water-fowls and seed-fowls, but of his kind—even to such interchanges of amenities as he had often heard along the Thames. And for the second time Chaucer's approach to human life has been through the medium of birds, as at the zenith of his powers he comes back to them again. For in that matchless trio of which the other members are Criseyde and the Wife of Bath, it is Madame Pertelote who makes the third.

The last, if not the greatest, of the visions poems, the Prologue to the Legend of Good Women, I must regretfully pass over, together with the Knight's Tale, which, like the Troilus and Criseyde, preceded it. It is Chaucer's dealings in the Troilus with the *Filostrato* to which I wish to come, for in the Troilus, never again to lose its ascendancy, life came, like a mighty river flowing in.

From Machaut and his French contemporaries Chaucer had taken over a form which for him was relatively empty of content. In Boccaccio and Dante he found for the first time among his moderns architectonic powers which in the case of Dante were supreme, and which Boccaccio in narrative exercised with a master's skill. Moreover, in Boccaccio, and superlatively in Dante, the greatness of the form was inseparable from the richness of the content, and that content was now no longer interminable lucubrations in a vacuum, but men and women, and their actions and their fates. And in the *Filostrato* he found a story richer in possibilities than any on which he had yet exercised his powers. Into none had so many strands been woven by earlier hands, from its far-off inception in the *Iliad*, down through a provocative catalogue of names in Dares, to three of which Benoit, through one of those inscrutable promptings of genius which set in motion incalculable trains of consequence, had attached a story of faithless love. And then Boccaccio, through his own *Filocolo*, poured into it the passion of his long eventful intrigue with Maria d'Aquino. And as the inevitable consequence, his Criseida and Troilo and Pandaro *live*, as his Palamon and Arcita and Emilia never do. In the *Filostrato* Chaucer at last had flesh and blood to deal with.

What the *Filostrato* did, accordingly, was to awaken as nothing else yet had done, his own creative powers. For the Troilus is a magnificently independent reworking of Boccaccio's narrative, bearing to its original, indeed, a relation not unlike that in which *King Lear*, for example, stands to the earlier play. For Chaucer had thought deeply through Boccaccio's story before he set pen to parchment for his own.

Boccaccio's Criseida is a fair and fickle woman, conventional alike in her beauty and her faithlessness; Chaucer's Criseyde, in her baffling and complex femininity remains unrivalled, save in Shakespeare and one or two of the great novelists. And by a change as simple as it is consummate in its art, Chaucer opened the way for another transformation —the metamorphosis of a conventional young man-about-town into a masterpiece of characterization which he equalled only, if I may hazard my own opinion, in the Wife of Bath. For Boccaccio's Pandaro was Criseida's cousin; Chaucer's Pandarus is her uncle. And through that simple-seeming shift, not only is the irony of the situation deepened and the tragedy enhanced, but Pandarus also becomes what a younger man could never have been—the vehicle of Chaucer's own humour and urbanity and worldly wisdom, and of his inimitable raciness of speech. Somewhere, among his courtly friends in England or in Italy or both, he had come, one feels, to know the type to which he gave immortal individuality. It is in the Troilus, too, that one also feels, again for the first time, that detachment which is also the distinctive note of the greater Canterbury Tales —that wise and urbane detachment with which Chaucer came in the end to view the human comedy. And often when Pandare speaks, one is curiously aware of something in the background—like Meredith's Comic Spirit with its 'slim feasting smile'—which is playing the game with Pandare no less urbanely and ironically than he with Troilus and Criseyde. And those are but hints of what Chaucer's reading of life lent to his reading of Boccaccio.

Moreover, no sooner had he set out to write than his mind began to race beyond the text he was translating. In scores of stanzas, even in the first book, he will follow Boccaccio for three or four or five lines of his stanza, then go his own gate for the rest of it, as if his thought in its eagerness overleaped Boccaccio's. And often, before he returns to his text, he has carried on alone for three, four, or a score of stanzas. And when, in the great second and third books, he comes to the heart of the drama as he conceives it, he leaves **Boc-caccio** almost wholly aside, and the great bulk of those **two** crucial books is Chaucer's own. And nowhere else, save **in** the plan of the Canterbury Tales, does he exercise **such** sovereign constructive powers. Life and his reading of **the** great Italians had made him master of his art.

And that mastery of an art which has for its end the por-trayal of life is peculiarly manifest in his dialogue. Let me read, if you will, a few of the stanzas which describe Pan-dare's visit to Criseyde's house:

> Whan he was come un-to his neces place,
> 'Wher is my lady?' to her folk seyde he;
> And they him tolde; and he forth in gan pace,
> And fond, two othere ladyes sete and she
> With-inne a paved parlour; and they three
> Herden a mayden reden hem the geste
> Of the Sege of Thebes, whyl hem leste.

> Quod Pandarus, 'ma dame, God you see,
> With al your book and al the companye!'
> 'Ey, uncle myn, welcome y-wis,' quod she,
> And up she roos, and by the hond in hye
> She took him faste, and seyde, 'this night thrye,
> To goode mote it turne, of yow I mette!'
> And with that word she doun on bench him sette.

> 'Ye, nece, ye shal fare wel the bet,
> If god wole, al this yeer,' quod Pandarus;
> 'But I am sory that I have yow let
> To herknen of your book ye preysen thus;
> For goddes love, what seith it? tel it us.
> Is it of love? O, some good ye me lere!'
> 'Uncle,' quod she, 'Your maistresse is not here!'

> With that they gonnen laughe, and tho she seyde,
> 'This romaunce is of Thebes, that we rede'. . .

> 'As ever thryve I,' quod this Pandarus,
> 'Yet coude I telle a thing to doon you pleye.'
> 'Now uncle dere,' quod she, 'tel it us
> For goddes love; is than th' assege aweye?
> I am of Grekes so ferd that I deye.'
> 'Nay, nay,' quod he, 'as ever mote I thryve!
> It is a thing wel bet than swiche fyve.'

'Ye, holy god!' quod she, 'what thing is that?
What? bet than swiche fyve? ey, nay, y-wis!
For al this world ne can I reden what
It sholde been; som jape, I trowe, is this;
And but your-selven telle us what it is,
My wit is for to arede it al to lene;
As help me god, I noot nat what ye mene.'

'And I your borow, ne never shal, for me,
This thing be told to yow, as mote I thryve!'
'And why so, uncle myn? why so?' quod she.
'By god,' quod he, 'that wole I telle as blyve;
For prouder womman were ther noon on-lyve,
And ye it wiste, in al the toun of Troye;
I jape nought, as ever have I joye!'

It would be hard to find even in the Canterbury Tales a
more superb handling of dialogue than that, with its swift
touch and go of actual talk, its subtle *nuances*, and its seeming
impromptu which only a master's technique could achieve.

And in nothing that he ever wrote did his possession at
once of the scholar's and the artist's gifts stand him in
better stead than in his weaving into one the complex
strands which underlay his story. And as he wrote, phrases
and ideas, Boccaccio's or his own, kept calling up to his
memory associated fragments of his reading, and the *Divine
Comedy*, and the *Convito*, and the *Teseide*, and a sonnet of
Petrarch, and Ovid, Virgil, Statius and Boethius, and the
*Roman de la Rose* and the *Roman d'Eneas* and even Machaut
himself (to name no more) contribute to the sense which we
have in the Troilus of a richness like God's plenty, which
pervades the poem.

When Chaucer ended the Troilus, he was in possession of
a mastered art. To the question which I asked in the
beginning—What aside from genius made the poet of the
greater Canterbury Tales?—I have attempted, within my
limits of time and understanding, to give an answer. The
supreme art of that crowning achievement had been learned
through the independent exercise of his own powers upon
given materials—upon form and content of conventional

types or specific poems, which the accident of courtly
connexions or business in Italy had offered. And through
the poet's gift of seeing the latent possibilities in everything
he touched, and through the scholar's passion for facts, and
through his own invincible eagerness of spirit which spared
no pains, his masters and his models slipped steadily into the
background, and on the threshold of the Canterbury Tales
the theme towards which his face was turned was *life*—that
life above all which through years of intimate contact with
it he had learned to know; not French life nor Italian life,
but English. And instead of any longer filling empty forms
or reconstructing full ones, he drew straight from life a
framework of his own—the one form in all the world to
give free play to his disciplined and ripened powers, and
room for all that wealth of reading and experience with
which this tale began. And as if with one lingering look
behind, he begins his masterpiece—I wish I knew whether
he so meant it—with an exquisite *ave atque vale:*

> Whan that Aprille with his shoures sote
> The droghte of Marche hath perced to the rote,
> And bathed every veyne in swich licour,
> Of which vertu engendred is the flour;
> Whan Zephirus eek with his swete breeth
> Inspired hath in every holt and heeth
> The tendre croppes . . .

and on through the lovely lines still redolent of their April
freshness after five hundred years. That is the stock introduc-
tion—*sed quantum mutatus ab illo*—to a hundred love-vision
poems! But instead of ushering in Plaisance and Esperance
and Douce Pensée and their crew of fellow abstractions,
it opens the door of the Tabard Inn to Harry Bailly and the
Wife of Bath and the Miller and the Pardoner and their goodly
fellowship. There could be no better symbol than those opening lines of the continuity, through steadily maturing powers,
of Chaucer's art. And it is that continuity of evolution, up
to the full flowering of his genius in the Canterbury Tales,
that I have essayed to describe.